Sound It Out

Long Vowels

by Wiley Blevins
illustrated by Sean O'Neill

BOOKS™

Red Chair Press   Egremont, Massachusetts

Look! Books are produced and published by Red Chair Press:

Red Chair Press LLC   PO Box 333   South Egremont, MA 01258-0333

www.redchairpress.com

 FREE activity page from www.redchairpress.com/free-activities

Wiley Blevins is an early-reading specialist and author of the best-selling *Phonics from A to Z: A Practical Guide* from Scholastic and *A Fresh Look at Phonics* from Corwin. Wiley has taught elementary school in both the United States and in South America. He has written more than 70 books for children and 15 for teachers, as well as created reading programs for schools in the U.S. and Asia.

Publisher's Cataloging-In-Publication Data

Names: Blevins, Wiley. | O'Neill, Sean, 1968- illustrator.

Title: Long vowels / by Wiley Blevins ; illustrated by Sean O'Neill.

Description: Egremont, Massachusetts : Red Chair Press, [2019] | Series: Look! books : Sound it out | Includes word-building examples. | Interest age level: 004-008. | Summary: "Vowels can say their names: A-E-I-O-U. These vowel sounds can be spelled many different ways, including vowel teams. Readers discover how these long vowels and vowel teams can be used to build words."--Provided by publisher.

Identifiers: ISBN 9781634403399 (library hardcover) | ISBN 9781634403511 (paperback) | ISBN 9781634403450 (ebook)

Subjects: LCSH: English language--Vowels--Juvenile literature. | English language--Pronunciation--Juvenile literature. | CYAC: English language--Vowels. | English language--Pronunciation.

Classification: LCC PE1157 .B542 2019 (print) | LCC PE1157 (ebook) | DDC 428.13--dc23

LCCN: 2017963412

Illustrations by Sean O'Neill

Photo credits: iStock

Printed in the United States of America

0918 1P CGS19

Vowels can make short sounds. Vowels can make long sounds, too. These long vowels say their names.

A-E-I-O-U

Let's see what these vowels can do.

Table of Contents

A is the first letter of the alphabet. It's also the first vowel. Long A can be spelled in many ways.

b<u>a</u>k<u>e</u>   c<u>a</u>k<u>e</u>
r<u>ai</u>n   tr<u>ai</u>n
s<u>ay</u>   pl<u>ay</u>

All have
Long A.

Long **E** is a happy sound.
Say "E" and feel the smile.
Long E can be spelled
in many ways.

r<u>ea</u>d   r<u>ea</u>ch

h<u>e</u>   sh<u>e</u>

s<u>ee</u>   tr<u>ee</u>

All have Long E.

See, he reads.

Long **I** moves in the mouth.
Say "I" and feel it go up and
down. Long I can be spelled
in many ways.

bike   like

light   night

my   cry

tie   pie

All have Long I.

Long O is a surprise sound.
Say "O" and look at your
mouth. Oh my! It's shaped
like an O.
Long O can be spelled
in many ways.

boat   coat
home   hope
snow   grow
go   no no no

All have Long O.

Long U has a sound-alike word. That's right! It's <u>you</u>. Long U can be spelled in many ways.

c<u>u</u>t<u>e</u>   c<u>u</u>b<u>e</u>
m<u>u</u>sic   men<u>u</u>
f<u>ew</u>   resc<u>ue</u>

All have Long U.

Let's Build Words

Those are the five long vowels.

A-E-I-O-U

With long vowels, what can you do? You can build a word.

Let's try it.

Say the sound for <u>b</u>.

Now say the sound for <u>ee</u>.

Put the two
sounds together.

What word did you make?

AAAGGGHH!

It's a **bee**. And it's after
you and me.

See the bee!

Let's try another one.

Say the sound for t.
Now say the sound for ea.
Put the two sounds together.
What word did you make?

tea

Yum! So sweet.

Say <u>tea</u> again.
Add the sound for <u>m</u> at the end. What word did you make?

team

So jump up and scream.

Scream for the team!

Let's try one more. We'll start with a short word.

ran

This is what you did when you saw that bee!

Now change the vowel sound in <u>ran</u>. Go from short to long. How?

Change the letter <u>a</u> to <u>ai</u>. The vowel will now say its name. What word did you make?

rain

Grab an umbrella!

Now let's keep going.

Say rain.
Add the sound for t to the beginning. What word did you make?

train

Choo. Choo. Hop on!

One last try.

Say <u>train</u>. Change the letter <u>t</u> to <u>b</u>. What word did you make?

brain

Yes, you are so smart. That's what you use to read words!

Vowels can make short sounds.
Vowels can make long sounds, too.

These long vowels say their names.

A-E-I-O-U

Now you know what these vowels
can do.